A Mile of Kite String

a third collection of poems

by Dorothy Pope

A Mile of Kite String
First published in 2016

Published by Dorothy Pope,
10 Runnelfield, Harrow on the Hill, Mx HA1 3NY
www.dorothypope.co.uk

© Dorothy Pope 2016

The right of Dorothy Pope to be identified as author of this work has been asserted in accordance with Section 77 of the Copyright, Designs and Patents Act 1988

ISBN 978-0-9542719-2-3

Front cover photograph by Jake Davies

Printed and bound by CPI Group (UK) Ltd, Croydon, CR0 4YY

In Memory of Michael

and to John, Robbie and Gill

Contents

Prolonging	7
Dawn	8
Evening Orange	9
Kiss Me	10
He Would Have Been So Glad	10
A Toast	11
Snakes and Ladders	12
To John, Fifty-two Today	13
Music in the Church	14
Lunchtime Concert	15
The Boys are Back	16
Counter Terrorists	17
A Fortnight	18
Snow	19
Vintage Champagne	20
May	21
Not Seen Through Apple Boughs	22
Elsewhere	22
The Twenty-second of March	23
The Best Things	23
Ninety Per Cent Proof	24
Naturalist	24
Great Spotted Woodpecker	25
Window	26
Nowadays	27
Blue Tit	28
These I Have Loved	29
Bulbs	30
Devon	31
Going Back	32
Misunderstanding	33
Bubbles	34
Buttered Toast	35
The Corner Shop	36
The Shop That Isn't There	37
School Reunion	38
Church Youth Club 1950	39

3rd September 1939	40
Teddy Bear 1940	41
Carrots and Radishes	42
Sandcastles	43
Golf on the Somme	44
Competition 1918	45
Jersey War Tunnels	46
Surprised by Joy	47
Monday Mother	48
Well Met, Stepfather	49
Robert Anderson 1927-2015	50
September	50
Edward Thomas by Robert Frost	51
Teaching	51
The Ghost of Mr Edelman	52
Weekly	53
Map of My Mother	54
Autumnal	55
Mercy	56
Dylan Thomas Acrostic	57
How Are You Now, Poor Child I Did Not Help?	58
Unreconciled	59
South Devon	60
Swear-Words in the Play	61
Red Wellies, Aged Eighty	62
Life Begins at Ninety	63
Bad Marriage	64
Cinderella Rap	65
To His Coy Mistress (a version)	66
I Do Not Collect Owls	67
Squirrel	68
Autumn Joy	68
To See the Sea	69
Nostalgiad	69
Grammar Limericks	70
Adlestrop	71
Stopping by Woods on a Snowy Evening	71
The Listeners	71

Prolonging

I'm tying up these hyacinths, their blooms
top heavy, full as love, securing them
with knitting pins and short lengths cut off from
the mile of kite string you requested when
I asked your choice of anniversary gift,
the first of forty-nine. Oh how you flew
your kite! Now resurrected, you had left
it in the attic bedroom of your boyhood. New
conferred on our home, it made me feel
bestowed with utter trust that you could fly
alongside me. And so you did. I will
prolong these hyacinths' blue iris life,
bound to the needles, half a century old,
I used to knit for you when you were cold.

Dawn

and I will spin a thread of birdsong
and another one of morning light
and weave the fabric of a day.
I will pattern it with leaf dapple
and hang it, hammock, from an apple tree.

In the evening I will dye it
with the indigoes of twilight,
embroider it with countless stars,
and draw it, moonlit counterpane,
around your shoulders as you sleep.

Evening Orange

At half past eight, he'd pause. Selecting one
of seven mirrored on a kitchen plate
of tempered silver he alone had shone,
he'd start with ritual and delicate
and thorough care to peel not just the skin
but every bit of bitter pith outside
the separable segments in their thin
unruptured envelopes. When satisfied,
he'd probe each pair of engorged lips apart,
with keen, unsheathed and dedicated blade
and then arrange with skilled and practised art
each intact sliver. Every morsel laid
for her to relish, nightly compliment
when she came home, retained its juice held pent.

Kiss Me

Kiss me and my white hair's yellow.
Hold me and my thick waist's narrow.

Eye me and my tired step quickens.
Touch me and my youth awakens.

Meet my eyes and tensions soften.
Kiss me lovingly and often.

He would have been so glad

to see the chaffinch back,
the lilac thrive,
the peony come on,
the feared for rose alive -

that rose,
the one we chose
for redness, form and fragrance -
true lovers' rose.

A Toast

You wear your crown so lightly, Aristo.
One might have thought you must slip in and out
of genius to be a normal boy
but no, not separate selves, twin gifts that fuse.
Hardworking with no pre recital nerves,
no post performance need of rest,
exceptionally stable temperament
accompanies your talent happily.
So, as the serious magic of the music
of your flying fingers lingers on
as meditative afterglow, so does
the impress of your character, polite
and modest, calm and strong. To Aristo,
a prodigy who's also nice to know.

Snakes and Ladders

Here on the carpet
we played board games:
Ludo - I play,
Snakes and Ladders
and a third called Sorry,

this before you started school
where you did not play
but instead learned dread,
and endurance down ten years of snakes.
Sorry.

Sorry all my days
I failed to rescue you,

your only crime your innocence
encased in that pathetic shell
of cracked and bleeding,
itching eczema.

Now, in your bowed,
brave after years,
I beg your pardon
tender boy within

and wish you ladders,
many ladders,
and no more snakes.

To John, Fifty-two Today

I'd pushed it up the hill when full,
delivered all the wine I'd bought
as Christmas thank you gifts, and now,
light and downhill, it fairly bowled
along. I scarcely had to push.

I breathed the crisp December air
in fine contentment as I strolled,
my mind freewheeling dreamily.

My Blackwatch tartan shopping bag
became the high and well sprung pram
in gleaming cream and navy blue
of fifty long short years ago,
new baby lying snug inside.

And you aloft my two year old,
up, cheery, on the toddler's seat,
then memorably paraphrased
a salutation to a king
from one of all our fairy tales,
turned to your brother and declared,
"We greet you Robert. Long life to you."

Still marvelling, remembering,
I reached my home, garaged the Black-
watch tartan bag, let myself in
the house and made a cup of tea.

Music in the Church

Here where three ancient flagstone corners meet
there is a little lodging place just right
to keep a cello spike securely held.
Neat, handy, just the job, it fascinates
me. Was it there? Was it enlarged a bit
or gouged out with a mitigating prayer?
I like to know the ins and outs of things.

And now a boy is playing, fifteen years old,
shirt cuffs undone and folded back. Again,
I wonder. Why? For ease of playing? Or are
his sleeves just plain too short like those
of any growing boy at end of term?
Extraordinary ordinary boy
for he is playing like an angel. He

makes a cathedral of a parish church.
He coaxes and commands by turns such roars,
such throaty groans, such sweet and mellow moans,
high mewing pleas and aching sobs from out
the curving belly of his instrument
which rests safe in the place provided where
the corners of three ancient flagstones meet.

Lunchtime Concert

Violins, all haunting sad today,
reach deep into my anniversary blues
with incidental five note motif whose
recurring sorrowing runs all the way
through Schindler's List.   And as they play,
my sympathetic grieving for the Jews
stirs thoughts of him I loved and was to lose.
The music says what I was loth to say.
I, so reluctant to be touched at first,
preferring safety in my careful shell,
now find a soothing in a grief expressed
at one remove, as stroked by feathers, till
this glancing echo of the Holocaust,
embedded, eases me, makes me more well.

The Boys Are Back!

Throughout the weeks of August's length,
the pavements top of Harrow Hill
deserted, the occasional
old lady, thin in her great age,
selects each slow and careful step,
the fifty quiet yards ahead
without a second soul.

                    And then -
September and the boys are back!
In twos and threes and sauntering
yet purposeful in nonchalance,
peopling the hill again,
suffusing it with youthfulness,
haircut and serious smile apiece,
our own dear blazered boys are back.

Counter-Terrorists

I'm sitting on a low brick wall
to witness boys as they run past
me up a long steep hill, the last
half mile of twenty mile run -
Albert Memorial and back for charity:

the boy who played the oboe solo,
this for charity, at ten
o'clock last night, only to rise
at five, today before the race,
a clarinettist too. He smiles and waves.

One boy, his left arm in a sling,
makes nothing of his handicap,
elbows the air and keeps on straight.
The overweight are short of breath,
show greater stress but gamely struggle on.

The fittest run alone it seems.
The second best do best in twos.
None are untouched, unchallenged by
this pushing of themselves so far,
so hard, heroically for charity.

Four hours now and they're spaced out:
the ones, the twos, the threes, the groups.
Sweat-soaked white tee-shirts flag the way
the long hill down and still they come.
I think, "Thank God for good boys. Still they come."

A Fortnight

Winter came early, sudden and severe.
It had been such a perfect autumn too,
exceptionally sunny all the year.
But then, inside a little fortnight, you
and all October's goldenness were gone.
There was no warning gradualness. Grief
came not as gentle schooling, nor upon
our oak was left a solitary leaf.
Its boughs were skeletal against the skies.
In fourteen days your face was gaunt and thin.
Though death was new to us, your haunted eyes
told unmistakably what grew within
you. Two short weeks can rob a man of life,
can strip an oak, make widow of a wife.

Snow

Back then, in snowman-building time, both
sexagenarian and unafraid,
safe in love's sapphire anniversary days,
when wrapped in happiness and overcoats,
yours a blue-grey, exact match for your eyes,
we wrote our love in footprints in the snow,
fed garden birds, laughed, photographed, so
larked in snowfall's rare and temporary delights,
I almost never dreamt such bliss would cease,
that one December diagnosis day,
I'd write stunned semicolon upside down, old
friends who came with Christmas gifts for us
could seem irrelevant, elsewhere, I'd say
the snow fell spectral, desolate and cold.

Vintage Champagne

They laid down joy like summer wines,
not consciously but having and to spare,
and gave it freely to their family, friends,
abundant though it was so fine and rare
but all the time the sparkling richness flowed,
someone, somewhere, a jealous ledger kept.
It was as though they must repay, they owed.
The books must balance. As they'd laughed, they wept.
Few cellared, dusty bottles now reside.
They're drunk in flights of sweet remembering
when someone lets her talk of him with pride,
or someone else does. Then her spirits sing.
But these rare toasts the grieving memory begs.
Mostly, her parched lips must make do with dregs.

May

Rosebuds, foxgloves and columbines today.
White lilac blooms persist, huge, double, snowy,
fragrant, though the glorious one is over now,
the rich dark purple Roi Charles Treize.
With their improbable lush pink display,
tree peonies prolong exotic pomp
while their less showy cousin splits its plump
white dumpling buds. They were the deepest red
when they moved in but bled their crimson
through the years in tandem tears shed
as loving woman wept for him who planted
that red rose above it on the fence
which, opening out this morning as she sat
reliving memories, blessed her with its scent.

Not Seen Through Apple Boughs

I used to watch you from this summerhouse,
your thinness stretched up to a branch to fill
the peanut feeder for the birds. I still
look through the leafy tracery, slim boughs'
green lace, but while this filligree allows
the fretted view beyond, no white shirt will
appear and move, no form of you distil.
My vision blurs but memory endows
my morning haunt with sharp and focused thought.
Unkind to take the man and not the need
of him. Bless me with both, take both away;
this way is amputation, leaves my heart
in rawest agony to weep and bleed.
I peer in vain. You'll not be there today.

Elsewhere

I bought a dozen of this birthday card -
two kittens, beautiful, "From both of us"
inscribed above the lovely photograph.
No use for these now. Time to face my loss,

give them to a friend whose husband's there,
who nightly occupies the other chair.

The Twenty-second of March

I'm seeing the swing
that isn't there any more
with a sweet limbed boy
alternately urging and idling it
playing Daffodil Journey
facing and trusting his brother
who's steering a rope hung tyre
to his right then his left,
swing and tyre securely provided
by the man
who is also not there,
his white shirt obscured
by a plum blossom mist.

The Best Things

in life are free. Yes, so I'm told.
The facile platitude of old
tells me to mind not money much:
possessions and position - such
but, here's the rub, I never did.
What then for me who sit amid
the ruins in this widowhood?
He was my free. He was my good.
The proverb's hollow, glib and grim.
I only ever wanted him.

Ninety Per Cent Proof

I thought I'd been so clever. Not for me
chance woundings by the million triggers. Proof
is what I planned, was sure that I would be
against the random darts but I, aloof
in my preparedness, could not have known
I had a chink, was vulnerable too.
One line of script and I was overthrown.
Although banal and bald, it pierced me through:
hurt blurting from new widower in the plot,
"One day you're married. Then one day you're not".

Naturalist

and when he died,
two gardens to his credit,
he left the seed of his philosophy
in those who followed on.

Great Spotted Woodpecker

How often he told me the difference -
juvenile, female and male.
It's the red bits that tell you:
crown, back of head dab or none.

I wish I'd remembered
but there seemed no urgency then
as I squandered his knowledge
carelessly sure that he'd always be there.

So, woodpecker, here we are -
you unidentified, me unaccompanied,
sharing his garden,
the roses deposed
by chrysanthemum and berry.

Window

Framed picture, posed for most of every day,
defying the impossible with ease,
resourceful, speculating, hungry jay
alights for want of chopped down damson trees,
learns how to perch and cling on to the mesh
suspended peanut basket, there to feed
and gracefully display his blue wing flash,
near nonchalant about contented greed.
Books say jays cannot vertically perch,
and knowledgeable friends pause in surprise.
True, first attempt was horizontal lurch
but this was soon perfected; he grew wise.
And as I watch, I mark and marvel, rapt,
think to be schooled how seamlessly adapt..

Nowadays

I shall not run or dance again, or even
sit or lie in peace, not spring from chair,
with unpremeditated joy embrace,
not lift a child, or walk a mile, or cross a carefree room.

But I remember suppleness that was
so clearly that in dreaming I still move
with ease and grace, the body partner to
the wish, in skylark meadows of my memory.

Each footstep, turn and gesture now I find
has felt balletic echo in my unhurt mind.
In the winter of my injury there remain
held summers which engender patience and sustain.

Blue Tit

Mere half an ounce of pollen dusted blue,
more than your every gaudier counterpart
you softly charmed your way into my heart
and came to be my icon. It is true
that I've rejoiced in every bird that flew
in here to swing with high gymnastic art
on wire mesh basket. Each balletic dart
for peanut feeding thrilled. But it was you.
Ten eggs to hatch, ten chicks to feed then fledge,
your modest colours faded as you tired.
You lost your mating bloom, your plumage frayed
with countless flights from nuts to nest via hedge-
row watch. I've sympathised and I've admired
you, tiny bird, such huge impression made.

These I Have Loved

A blue tit on the kitchen window sill,
green shoots that tell me that the daffodil
dismisses winter, that the filigreed
trees will leaf up, that spring is guaranteed,
warm sunshine on the skin, soft lifted hair
in gentle breeze, all these are free as air:
a turquoise sea in soothing synchrony
or in its pewter mood of savagery,
the evening robin as it shouts its bounds
and other, comforting domestic sounds -
and smells - returning family's key in lock,
its click, their greeting I have watched the clock
for, Sunday roast aroma, appetite to match,
son's likeness to his father such that I catch
my breath, trust in men of integrity
and life itself, miraculous and free.

Bulbs

Exploring, one day, near Shoreditch,
I came upon a church in which
some bright, enlightened soul had said,
"Henceforth, commemorate our dead
a different way. Let's have no more
of graves but flowers by the score,
a hundred say, the going rate -
of crocuses - to celebrate
the lives of loved ones. Let's adorn
this place in memory, not mourn."

In springtime now, they bloom in drifts
of thousands, and one's spirit lifts -
an inexpensive, grand idea.
What simple genius was here.

Devon

I do not think it is alone that I
was born there and was happy as a child,
was parented, built sandcastles and dreams,
that Devon rhymes with heaven. It is wild

and mildly beautiful, its beaches safe
with playful waves. They curve and wrap you round.
But if white water is more to your taste
then a more rugged canvas can be found.

That brooding, dark, outstripping, awesome moor
surprises primrose glades, the violet, full
streams that laugh and gurgle over boulders.
Pause. Flirt dangled foot. Restore your soul.

How Devon ripens blackberries! How red
its earth. With what timing and dramatic art
bestows its coast at Dawlish from that train.
How Devon calls and aches my London heart.

Going Back

When we went there together, those great stones,
right awful in their majesty, stood stark,
alone and grand as we looked round, their groans
of ages almost audible, their dark
commanding shapes, a church in which we stood
in awe, respect a natural response.
This time, I went alone and thought I would
recapture that grave mood that we'd known once

but found Stonehenge - Stonehenge! - quite dwarfed.
Those mystic whispers went unheard for din,
our great upthrusting monoliths roped off
against those for whom a theme park would have done,
in case a million pushes by brash kids
would loosen them like teeth, their silhouettes
no longer outlined on the sky - ye gods! -
competing with the car park loos instead.

Misunderstanding

On Christmas morning nineteen thirty-eight,
I woke to extra magic. I'd believed
their talk of Santa, tree and presents but
no one had mentioned snow. On Christmas Eve
the world had been its usual brown and green.
This morning every outside inch was white.
Knee deep, this stuff, my first, and only seen
in books. The crisp of it! The cold, the wet,
the everywhere of it, to touch, to marvel,
tramp your boots a track of six inch prints
and see the coal and dustbins beautiful.
I registered this rare coincidence
as guaranteed, expected it next year.
Though Christmas came, the snow failed to appear.

Bubbles

On Sunday, when she wasn't tired,
she'd set aside some time for me
and with transparent, oval soap,
blow bubbles in my bath. I'd see
her magically transform the foam,
with thumb and index finger so
stretch out an iridescent skin
that it was possible to blow,
with gradual and greatest care,
enormous bubbles! Beautiful!
I'd will them not to burst. They'd grow
as big as champion marrows till
they did. Then she would blow me more,
each floating lovelier than the others.

This labelled jar boasts, "Bubble Bath"
but gifts no bubbles like my mother's.

Buttered Toast

Always on cold winter evenings
I would be in charge of toast -
long brass fork and fire of embers -
doing what I loved to most.

Chink of knife on plate through butter
then the rasp as it was spread,
melting on to dribbled chin then
drink of milk and off to bed.

Unmomentous and domestic
memories you'd think would fade
yet they are the stuff of childhood
and the comfort of old age.

The Corner Shop

A feature of my childhood map
along with powdered eggs and Zubes,
with threepenny bits and Oxo cubes
and wire-cut cheese and hand carved ham,

a row of glass-topped biscuit tins,
blue handmade sugar-paper bags
for groceries scooped out of sacks,
and dry goods shovelled out of bins,

such handy things as nibs and chalk,
by sweets in jars and pins and tape,
and butter patted into shape
with lots of time to stand and talk.

Our corner shop is long since gone
fast food, computers and junk mail
and supermarkets now prevail
and my map lines are quite redrawn..

The Shop That Isn't There

A few yards from the school yard gate
was Madame Wilson's, Corsetiere,
and I was sent there from age eight
two or three times every year

to pick up Miss Black's corselette
(a corset topped off with a bra),
a pale pink garment of some weight.
The bones made it a cylinder

and later showed in ridges through
her crêpey dresses - mauve and green.
Slim gym-slipped junior's incongru-
ity, thus burdened, seldom seen!

Sedate, dim shop with pinging wire,
to whizz the change back down, complete,
has disappeared with its attire.
So has my school. So has the street.

School Reunion

Slim gym slip girls, if we'd foreseen
what needs of courage lay ahead,
would we have blessed clairvoyancy
or lived our golden years in dread?
With troubles spooned out, surely we
are gently schooled, can graduate,
absorb each shock's reality
down sixty years of random fate,
as trials come singly, in a while
the wisdom of the brave face knowing
through pain and disappointment, smile
the nobility of keeping going.
We skylark girls were mercifully
ungifted with clairvoyancy.

Church Youth Club 1950

School dress, yes, but socks off,
Mother's stockings on
with birthday high heeled shoes
and Yardley's lipstick -
English Rose - and powdered nose.

Fifteen, and days at school
mere interludes, Tuesdays the thing
for table tennis and Beethoven's Fifth
till Spin the Bottle
and The Harry Lime Theme
when the married minister gave us the key.
He left early then for hanky panky
of his own with Miss Linnell,
reluctant spinster of that parish,
seen arm in arm with him
in Leamington one afternoon.

Though near impossibly shy,
I learned the how and why
of kissing: you could breathe
and noses did not pose a problem,
not at all.

How in the year we all paired off
for puppy love
except for lovesick Shirley Jones
whose heart throbbed for a film star
she did not know was homosexual
and nor did we
nor had we heard of such a thing
that year, our year
of boys and poor exam results.

3rd September 1939

                    and then with slow solemnity,
the utterance that was to change the world.
My mother fled to hide her sobs from me
and have some adult moments uncontrolled.

It had been such a peaceful morning too:
I with my measles, sofa-bound, content,
her intermittent sitting, us in tune,
our universes parallel. She went.

I wondered what these two words meant, to me,
new minted, juxtaposed, today. I'd heard
the "German" of my measles, "Germany",
mysteriously powerful wireless word.

Alone, and fractious suddenly, I lay
back, thought I'd find that out another day.

Teddy Bear 1940

Alone of my neglected teddy-bears,
the little blue and white old favourite shares
this fifth auspicious year in my affairs.
I comfort him in cupboard under stairs
or in the dark, cold Anderson if there's
enough of warning to come down. He stares
at me with fear in his glass eyes but wears
the scarlet scarf I knitted him and glares
up at the drone of Nazi bombers, squares
up, red, white and blue, in his contempt, dares
them to do their German worst, see if he cares,
sometimes, like Dad and Gran'pa even swears.
He'll be all right. But still he whispers prayers.

Carrots and Radishes

Before the fall, the twin great falls,
I had a garden one yard square,
prepared and sowed it, tended it
attentively. With minute care
and solemnly, I watered it,
twice daily scanned for signs my seeds
had "germinated" (fine new word!),
waged war on brash, invading weeds.

September nineteen thirty-nine
sowed first unease and then neglect -
another new word: "Germany".
I listened, watched, came to detect
what adults thought to keep from me.
I'd anyway learnt how to read.
My radishes grew woody, long,
my carrot tops browned, went to seed.

Momentously, I started school.
Of greater moment came The Blitz.
I realised a house could fall,
how marriage could be fragile, its
serenity a thin façade,
a brittle thing that cracked and broke.

These days, I have a garden. Though
its carrots, radishes evoke
my childhood one, the difference is
a marriage solid as an oak.

Sandcastles

With pail and spade she reconstructed house
and school, cathedral, sweet shop, and with shells,
she peopled them with parents, teacher, toys
and friends beneath unthreatening skies of gulls
that softly cried the grief she'd not expressed.
And when they saw the waters coming in,
they gently dusted her of sand and dressed
her, took her home, for she must not again
experience what tides of history could steal
for ever. Settled here and cleansed of dread,
she paddled in the playful waves with squeals
which nowadays were of delight. In bed,
tucked, lulled, she breathed, in sleeping synchrony,
the soothing music of the rhythmic sea.

Golf on the Somme

I came to find his name on Menin Gate
and play golf on that special ground but found
I heard on every fairway, green and tee
the silent screams, the rumbling guns, could see
in my mind's eye, the bloodshed all around.
Though poised to putt, I could not concentrate.

A shambles, massacre, Triangle Wood,
now Hole Thirteen - is this where Grandpa fell?
Hole Three, known as Our Lord's Tree - there, an oak
resprouted as Christ crucified. My stroke
was off as I paused, thought what kind of hell
was there, how that regrowth's symbolic good.

Eye level, nicely placed, I found his name,
in Ypres, at evening heard the last trumpet,
considered whether playing golf is quite
acceptable here where so many died,
decided yes but not, for me, quite yet.
Like him, because of him, I lost the game.

Competition 1918

The post war competition for young men
for husbands had not ever been as tough.
So many were not coming home again.
In plain terms there were simply not enough.

And "plain" is here the operative word.
Though sisters, we were quite unlike for you,
you were so pretty, I so plain. I heard
it said so often, knew it to be true.

Miraculously, Edwin, home from war,
chose me to court. I thought I had a chance
of love, knew joy, had hopes, but then before
it could take hold, you sundered our romance.

You toyed with him for idle vanity.
Your shallow conquest once achieved, you left
him soon, moved on and married one of three
you had to choose from, whereas I, bereft,

went on to live a life of spinsterhood,
became an aunt, was known as plain but good.

Jersey War Tunnels

A sound recording of an air raid's first -
Luftwaffe overhead. In Coventry?

An iron thunder hammers nerves with noise:
the whistles then explosions of the bombs

and anti aircraft guns' reply to planes
that fill the searchlit sky and grind the night.

I flinch at every bang, am taken back,
exhausted, teased by every jerked response,

assure my sons that this dark hell is true;
for forty nights The Blitz was just like this.

They note the authenticity with care
and seem to look at me with different eyes.

I, who could not afford to cry, aged five,
aged eighty, find my face is wet with tears.

Surprised by Joy

Who before you conducted symphonies
in my suburban living room,

declared Rachmaninov impossible
(you'd pierce the ceiling with your bow),

inspired me to empathise, find you
a pillow filled with softest down?

You made me want to rise at 4 a.m.
to see you off to France to play.

You charm the Yorkshire pudding off my plate
donating carrots in return,

reply you want to spend your twenty-first
with me, what's more, call this house "home".

Far from your fatherless, strict boyhood home,
on scholarship among the rich,

with mandarin looks and language, brave, adrift,
you moved my heart to tenderness.

I thought to give - but find myself endowed
with unimagined, rosy joy.

Monday Mother

White wash in copper, mangled and pegged out,
a stiff breeze fills the shirts with seven men,
the sheets and pillow slips to sailing ships,
the groaning, wooden, goose-beaked prop in place.

Her basket full of coloureds, pegs in teeth,
she fights the wind, replacing damp-dry whites.

While first flat iron comes to spit sizzling heat,
she washes kitchen lino-parquet floor
with saved remaining, cooling soapy water

then contests the whole week's waiting wash
with vigour banged irons, relays from the trivet.

Tribute to her, all now hangs on airer
hauled to ceiling height and she addresses
Sunday joint, cold beef, with carving knife,
and magics up crisped bubble and squeak in pans.

Dishes, wireless, knitting, cocoa, bed.

Well Met, Stepfather

He was the very Falstaff of a man,
hard drinking and hard playing, up most nights
in Mother's kitchen after pubs had closed
around the table playing cards with mates.

He'd greet her with a smacking buss when she
came down and, arm affectionately round
her aproned, trim behind, beam up at her,
"Your ham and eggs, m'wench, you'd be so kind,"

and she'd indulge him, somehow, as she cooked,
restoring order: glasses, ashtrays, cleared away,
smoke out and morning fresh air in till all
was sweet and clean for the new day.

Then he and all his chums tucked into food
and downed great mugs of tea before they said
goodbye till next time, thanking his good wife,
and he slept in contented feather bed.

Now dead and spared more of the agonies
of wasted body in heroic pain
by final closing time, the memories
of bonhommie and charm are what remain.

Robert Anderson
1927-2015

Not for him mere bread and circuses.
He determined his earned wealth be put
to charitable use. And so he formed
The Trust, his money and fine London house
providing for impoverished young men,
a rent-free room as rescue or as home
to make a course of study possible.

His own frugality contrasted
with the privilege he conferred, the treasures
of his learned mind, his author's scholarship -
of course, the archaeology and music
knowledge of exceptional range and depth -
but wisdom too and courtesy and wit
in kitchen conversations famed among friends.

September

Acorns again -
lying in the grass
or bombing the flat roof
of the classroom
where I'll help these children
to grow into oaks.

Edward Thomas by Robert Frost

Heedless to all but what you saw as set -
your passion to put poems on the page,
and volunteering, needless at your age -
you gave your life, it seemed, without regret
to these. And now your wife and children grieve:
Helen adoring spouse of such forbearance,
son, daughters lacking both their parents,
Mother inconsolable. You leave
me poorer too. Our talking walks were good.
You saw significances, thrashed them out
with typically tortured joy. I thought
you paid too high a price and wished you could
know ease of mood, my friend, **and** be inspired,
more, that you'd not died young, abroad, in war,
but here, and gently of old age, when tired.

Teaching

It's the light in the eyes
as understanding dawns
and clears the mists of misery.
That's what it's about.

The Ghost of Mr Edelman

Well into his eighties then, he told me once
how nicely he'd arranged his post retirement life -
up late, he'd breakfast with the Telegraph, set off,

there in the country house hotel, enclosed
in rhododendrons, a librettist's former home,
he'd take his place and play from twelve till half past two,

in continuous medley of their favourites,
his fingers travelling down the diners' years,
lighthearted music coursing through the meal,

how after that, he'd pick his daughter's girls
up from their schools, grandfathering until
their mother came, relieved him of their liveliness.

I dined in the Gilbert restaurant recently
and heard that pleasant stream of melodies,
searched, found the old piano in an alcove.

The eerie keys were moving up and down
to some invisible punched paper programme,
the stool not just unoccupied but gone.

Weekly

Weekly, after hours spent
in misery and rage,
rehearsing what she'd say,
she rose, unslept and unresolved.

Dodging him had never worked.
Now practised, she could usually
ward off his kissing
with a programme swiftly interposed
but his hands were quick
and if avoided,
came from behind her as she left.

Could she confront him
with her little speech this week?
She always failed to utter it,
to still the flutter in her voice,
could never quite remember it.

How could it be so difficult,
week in, week out impossible,
to tell the predatory priest

to keep his hands off her,
and not to kiss her any more?

Map of My Mother

Until today, I would have been hard put
to find words to epitomise her but
that was before I put the map back up.

My father years ago had had the job
of hanging it. He'd humped and hefted, lined it up
and screwed it on, she, shouldering to help

while he had strained and grunted, softly sworn.
Problem enough to take it down, I'd found.
Wallpaper and carpet workmen having gone,

the blank wall loomed at me expectantly.
Remounting of the huge steel map now fell to me.
I did it with bad grace. Reluctantly.

Today, with much to do when I got home,
a heavy week behind, ahead, I'd groaned
and cursed her bloody map. When it was done,

she beamed such happy thanks as quite disarmed
me. Then, with undiminished girlish charm,
said, "There! Now we can find Turkmenistan!"

Autumnal

Blown beeches squandering their lovely gold,
I, lordly rich with hoarded chestnut treasure,
glossed mahogany, abundant pocketfuls,
all down the coppery October hours
until the low sun squints the dwindled day,
boots pushing paper leaves back home
to evening cocoa jug, the fire glow
polishing the dresser, porridge papered walls
a dance of shadows, flickered flames of hearth
and fendered brass, the chill of bedtime stairs
warmed through by bless of blankets as the night
owl ushers in my patchwork dreams.

Mercy

At some hour in the middle of the night
(I could not know the time
save that my thirst confirmed
the thirty hours since my last drink
and when I had been bladder drained),
flat on my back in total, silent dark,
the seven-inch butchery of my abdomen,
re-sealed, I later saw,
with sharp-toothed, metal bulldog clips,
hurting brutally,

a tiny torchlight
and two disembodied presences.
One spoke.

"I'm going to give you something for the pain."
"A drink, too, please," my dry tongue rasped.
"No drink or you'll be sick."
"I'm never sick, I promise. Water, please."
"At breakfast. Now go back to sleep."

The little light and they were gone.

Helpless, I lay in unslaked wakefulness,
parched in the lonely dark.
It had, apparently, to be endured,
this agonising thirst.
But how? And for how long?
It was not nearly dawn.
Post anaesthetic
there's no appetite for sleep.

And then, alone this time,
the other presence, sweeter, still in the dark,
was back and whispering my name
and "I'm going to slip some ice chips in your mouth.
Please don't tell sister what I've done."

In all the forty years since then
I've not forgotten
those cold trickles of relief
nor my unidentified
good, brave nurse.

Dylan Thomas Acrostic

Daylong about my business which was play,
Young in the years of all my dreams,
Long-lolling the grass-sweet afternoons away,
Abundant was time and I was rich.
Nightlong too the wandering world was mine,
Time all I had but it was mine.
Headlong I ran my carefree course as king
Of buttercup fields and ferny woods,
Mountains and tumbling midnight streams.
And all my livelong days of reigning waned
Slowly till the swift years of my nowadays.

How Are You Now, Poor Child I Did Not Help?

Far up the beach and out of reach
of highest tides and danger lay
a paddling pool for children
three and four years old to play in
watched by mothers and the public
from a low surrounding wall

and here, where it should have been safe,
a perfect beauty of a dainty girl child,
barely four years old,
was suffering agonies she dare not name -
her shame: shy and bewildered eyes,
tense, tentative and troubled steps
a travesty of paddling,
embarrassment.

The infants, all save her,
wore trunks and swimsuits.

This little girl was naked,

paraded for her mother's gross
proclaiming of her own lost beauty
and her liberated attitudes.

"There's no such thing
as a consenting child!"
I wanted to protest.
"She longs for covering
like the rest of us.
She is suffering!"

Thirty pairs of staring eyes now probed
what should have been her own,
now pitifully, cruelly exposed.

Through closed lips came
a wild-eyed silent scream
of thinnest sensitivity.

I witnessed all, and I,
too ill for confrontation, my excuse,
did nothing, twenty years ago.

Unreconciled

I can forgive all the others
what they did to me
but not Miss Black
for what she did to Maudie Jenkins.

One junior afternoon,
as we were stitching aprons
in unsuspecting innocence,

she, in nothing but her lust
for punishing,
ordered Maudie out to the front
and then to lie down in the sewing hamper,
two thirds full with handwork stuck with pins,
then fastened down the lid.

Maudie wet herself in that dark place,
her only crime her low intelligence,
her poverty and physical deformity.

Surely a betrayal of that poor child
if I were reconciled to that.

South Devon

South - the very word is a caress -
long, leisured vowel and consonants that kiss
with sibilant and final breath-like sigh,
onomatopoeic epithet,
well conjured euphony, appropriate
for Devon's always gentle loveliness.
Perhaps one's place of birth leaves its impress
and at each christening, godmother-like,
attends to touch and bless the child so that
he will admire, his thinking will reflect
that county's character. The tenderness
of Devon's climate, south coast shelteredness,
September fruit and sun-warmed walls alike,
quiet glades of primrose and of violet,
gave me a love of all things temperate.

Swear-Words in the Play

Their faces as delighted laughter burst
from them reminded me of plums that split
with pressure of an unplucked readiness.

A school trip class of boys eleven years old
accompanied by teachers sitting near,
they heard the sergeant's words in disbelief.

"Stop goin' on about your effin' 'orse!
Now what do I not want to 'ear no more
about?" "My effin' 'orse Sarge, effin' 'orse."

So could they really laugh at this - out loud -
they wondered to each other, saucer-eyed.
It seemed they could, and heartily they did.

Small boys do not exactly slap their thighs.
They rocked and heaved in young equivalent
and, when the laughter in the house and theirs

subsided, sighed in happy satisfaction,
beamed their agreement down the line that life
could surely hold no greater joy than this.

Red Wellies, Aged Eighty

"You'll **never** wear them!" one friend said.
Another mentioned mutton. "Red!"
they said, "At your age! Really!" So
I stood them in the cloakroom though
still unconvinced they were a crime
against good taste, viewed them each time
I chose a raincoat, never wore
them, still, because of friends, unsure.

And then it snowed! Six inches deep.
"Ha ha," I thought, "my boots will keep
me dry," and strode to Waitrose, met
my friends. Both, with cold feet and wet,
said, "Sorry, will you tell us, please,
where we can buy good boots like these?"

With merest Mona Lisa smile,
I passed on down the dry goods aisle
with airy model's lack of haste.
"I'll teach them to impugn my taste,"
I thought and bought defiant jellies:
two raspberry ones to match my wellies.

Life Begins at Ninety

Yes, life begins at ninety. It is true.
You get excused all kinds of nasty chores
like washing dishes. As for gardening you
just say you're far too frail, must stay indoors.

You do feel up to telly, food and games,
describing how life was between the wars.
Pretending to be deaf or daft are claims
which never fail to silence crashing bores.

Come lunch-time, you can leg it to the table
then aver that indigestion gives you pause.
A large postprandial brandy gets you stable
before **the** most uninhibited of snores.

At half past three, you rouse for tea. You've found
that exercise is best kept to the jaws.
At ninety you're so proud to be around,
you think you're due a big round of applause.

Bad Marriage

Odd, ill-assorted pair, they chafed
like badly fitting shoes,
had blistering rows of rage and hatred
laced with insults whose
spiked venom was supposed to make
the other toe the line
or come to heel, fall into step,
thus gain the upper hand

but had the opposite effect.
They both went at it hell
for leather, buckled, came apart,
became divorced, to boot,
past any cobbler's art.

Cinderella Rap

While the mean ugly sisters upped an' went to the ball,
Cinderella stayed home goin' nowhere at all.
Now whichever way you figure it, that ain't nice
so the fairy godmother came an' made with the mice
an' the pumpkin, swanky dress an' shoes of glass,
sent Cindy to the venue looking real high class
sayin', "Leave at twelve honey. Watch the big clock well
cos midnight is the end of my magic spell."
So when the clock struck, Cindy cut and run
never mind she an' the prince were havin' so much fun.
But in her hurry to split, one dainty shoe'd
slipped off an' was found by the royal dude
an' he called at the houses, not some but all,
lookin' for the pretty lady he'd wooed at the ball.
The sisters' feet were too big though they squeezed
                                                and tried
but Cindy's fitted perfect so he made her his bride.

To His Coy Mistress
(a version)

Oh teasing and reluctant bint,
if I had time I'd do my stint
of waiting, serving my due term
while you delight to see me squirm
but move your arse, gal! Life is short!
Do give a gent a friendly thought.
I am an easy-going bloke
but frankly you're beyond a joke.
So what? You're beautiful, a joy
and I'm a fine upstanding boy;
much longer though and you will see
not Muscle Man but OAP.
 At least, not to exaggerate,
an impotency candidate.
So lie down, girl, and cut the bull.
You'll find it's bloody wonderful!

with of course acknowledgement
to Andrew Marvell

I Do Not Collect Owls

Asking for trouble, I suppose,
to put the first one, oddly given
by a dinner guest,
on a shelving complex
like a noughts and crosses blank
but with thirty-six compartments,
this a gift from someone else.

Subsequently, friends
have been filling up these squares
with owls: candidates of wood
and china, leather, felt and glass,
of alabaster, even silver.

There are twenty-seven owls now
in this assembled parliament
although, as I keep trying to say,
I do not, never have collected owls.

Squirrel

So like flight, your carefree leap
from one still trembling slender branch
to bending yet another low. You keep
me fascinated as you launch
yourself, consummate nonchalance.
I wonder is your journey planned
or do you not care where you land?

I don't know which I envy most,
your effortless gymnastic skill
or your sublime cool confidence,
unworried joy that you feel till
from sailing merrily aloft
you make your landing safe and soft.

Autumn Joy

A low October sun, slant
filtered through the gilded trees,
squints my eyes into a smile
that welcomes temperate autumn's
unexcessive weather, kinder light
and subtler colours,
cool, exhilarating air
that crisps the leaves
to spindrift gold
I push my shoes through
with remembered satisfaction.

To See the Sea

In a colander they went to sea.
Their friends predicted gloomily,
"You'll capsize, sink and drown, you'll see."
But they smiled optimistically.
They took a dozen balloons to buoy
them up and paper hats for joy
and safety pins, profiteroles
and chewing gum to stop the holes.
They told dry jokes when they got wet
and blew a tenor clarinet.
They visited exotic isles
and greeted people there with smiles.
When they got back with hearts aglow
their friends said, "There, we told you so."

Of course, with apologies to Edward Lear

Nostalgiad

Oh for a taste of Fuller's Walnut Cake!
Good as she is, my mother cannot bake
one that's a patch. I positively ache
to cut a slice and delicately take
a fingernail sized portion, just a flake
of that incomparable icing, make
its fragile eggshell crispness slowly break
down on my tongue, and blissfully partake -
translucent white, a tad short of opaque,
a work of genius and no mistake.
Though there are copies more than you could shake
a stick at, I can recognise a fake
at forty paces so, for pity's sake,
have mercy. Bring back Fuller's Walnut Cake!

Grammar Limericks

You lied or you lay or you laid?
Let me speedily come to your aid.
You laid tables and cables and plans,
lay in bed or your bath or on sands
and you lied about having got laid.

To the surgeon as he took his fees
(with ill-concealed glee), I said, "Please!
It's not the op that appals
but the labels on walls
with their wrongly used apostrophes!"

Three English mistakes I deplore -
I'll go further: the word is "abhor" -
are "could of" and "would of"
and then of course, "should of".
Please teachers, let's hear them no more.

Adlestrop   Edward Thomas

Train stopped.
Wonder why.
Nothing happened.
Nice sky.

Stopping by Woods on a Snowy Evening
Robert Frost

Stopped here.
Horse thought, "Queer!"
Great snow.
Gotta go.

The Listeners   Walter de la Mare

I arrived as arranged.
No-one there; bit strange.
Spooky feeling. Didn't dwell.
Rode off. Oh well.

Prolonging won second prize in an SWWJ competition
Evening Orange - published
Snakes and Ladders won first prize in an SWWJ competition
A Fortnight - a prize in an SWWJ competition
May appeared in Acumen
Elsewhere appeared in Poetry News
Bubbles was placed in an Oldie competition
Teddy Bear 1940 appeared in South magazine
Surprised by Joy appeared in Acumen
Edward Thomas by Robert Frost appeared in Acumen
I Do Not Collect Owls appeared in Poetry News
Adlestrop appeared in The Woman Writer
Stopping by Woods on a Snowy Evening - The Woman Writer
The Listeners appeared in The Woman Writer